Can I Speak?

by

Allen Levi Simmons

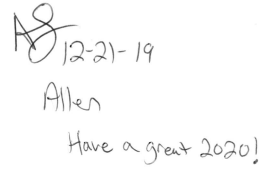

12-21-19

Allen

Have a great 2020!

ISBN: 978-0-578-59618-1

Can I Speak?

For permission requests, please contact the author via the "Contact" page on the following website: www.allenlevisimmons.com

Proudly self-published through Divine Legacy Publishing, www.divinelegacypublishing.com

Author's Note

After spending the past eight years recovering from PTSD, poetry has become the gateway to my peace. I have spent much time evaluating the effects of traumatic events stemming from broken families, alcoholic addictions, depression, and identity crisis.

When doctors and psychologists were unable to help me, and after going through prescribed pills from the Veteran's Hospital, I found that writing my thoughts onto paper or my cell phone was better than the drugs given to me.

Many times, people go through life and are told that they should trust the medicine. For some, it works; for others it makes life unbearable because we get so lost in the symptoms of our struggles and not the root of the problem.

I hope that the stories and poems within this book will empower you, provoke empathy, and inspire you to write your own book of poems. You will have the opportunity to read the thoughts that have been in my heart and mind over the last eight years. Thank you for taking the time to read the writings within this book.

Introduction

Believing that you are reading this because you are interested in learning about me, I choose to take you to a place. Follow my mind into this place, just for a moment.

Look around, smiling faces, women crying, children dying, and it seems as if no one is surviving. Welcome to my world! The sound of victory lingers in the wind with no one to hear its cry. Graves shout at nations because they are reaching full capacity and it's before everyone's time.

The face of a man is like a collage of photos; depending on which frame you choose to glance at, he's looking at a woman while she's looking at her husband. One frame down you see him with a coke bottle and his tenth bottle of crown. He seems happy in some frames. No one sees through the tainted surface of his heart. Deep down he feels pressure, he feels neglected; according to his bank account he's not respected.

Stop! Turn with me to this other corner.

Are you tired?

We've only caught a glimpse of the world we live in.

Failure

Don't let failure imprison your mind or bring scoliosis to your spine and leave you bent. You were born to be great and set aside to be great. Your every breath is more precious than diamonds and pearls; step out from this world and take a leap into your destiny. Look into the mirror and see what others cannot. You are unbreakable, place your feet on God's word and you will be unshakable. You are royalty; your royalty should be shown by how much you have grown. Seeds of failure and success have both been sown, but please don't step down form your throne. Keep marching, keep moving, you are almost home.

Did anyone tell you that your story was without meaning? Did anyone hear your dreams and instructed you to stop dreaming? If so, let them go. Let them see God take you from the valley into your promise land. Take my hands as I remove you from the quicksand. Fly with me! Gather your feathers and lift up your head. Aim for the stars with me. Stretch and reach the heights with me; we are survivors. Through train wrecks, car wrecks, broken bones, and life's test, we will all overcome.

Unbreakable people will be tested by pressures that measure their durability. Do you believe in God's ability? Do you believe in your ability? You are able to be all that you ever dreamed to be! No ears have heard, and no eyes have seen, all that God has for you and me.

Listen! Believe! Achieve! It is time, the time is now. Become unbreakable.

Motherless Child

Did you ever have a childhood superhero? Somehow superheroes give us more than hope, they reveal some greater purpose in life and can give hope to those who feel ostracized by society. Superman was my childhood superhero because of his strength. I think we all can admire the strength of a man who can lift up buses and give hope to people by saving them from an evil villain. I am certain that most of us have one or more evil villains in our lives. What if we lived in a world where we were all superheroes who saved others and ourselves from an enemy?

The sun was hiding behind a giant cloud as the day was coming to an end. The birds flew towards the sunset as the wind blew gently against the trees. A cold chill grew as the spring day felt like winter and the children were running into their homes for dinner.

"Oscar! Come inside before your dinner gets cold," his mother yelled from the kitchen window that faced the backyard.

Oscar was a seven-year-old boy who had golden brown skin and silky black hair that curled and would shine in the sun. He was the only brown boy in his neighborhood and a lot of children chose to play with each other and exclude Oscar in their daily games of hide and seek. He was alone in his backyard wishing he could disappear like the sun that was being covered by the clouds of the evening night.

"Oscar! Come inside before your dinner gets cold, I am not going to say it again!"

He took heed to his mother's demand and climbed out of the fort he'd made of sticks. His nails were filled with dirt because he had been entertaining himself with toy soldiers and superhero action figures, his favorite being Superman. Superman would fight off the other toys alone, kicking and punching them with the force from Oscar's hands guiding Superman in his fight against the wicked toy soldiers.

He left the toys and walked through the backdoor, wiping his feet on the doormat as his mother had instructed him many times before. The smell from the baked chicken lingered in the air and made its way into Oscar's nostrils and down to his stomach. The smell was so strong and delightful that he could taste the food before even seeing it. After washing his hands, he sat at the dinner table, and his mother brought the food on his favorite superhero plate, the one with a big S for Superman on the bottom of it.

"Did you remember to wash your hands?" his mother asked.

"Yes ma'am, I did," Oscar said as he hung his head down after another lonely day without friends.

"Mom, when can we go to the movies? We never do anything, and you are always leaving me with the babysitter."

She fixed her face in a stern way as she looked into her son's eyes as he slowly lowered his head and eyes toward his plate. He knew that his mom was getting ready to head out for the evening and she would be returning later in the night while he was in bed.

"Oscar, I need to go out because I need mommy time. I work every day, and I am stressed."

"Yes ma'am, I understand. I really miss spending time with you and dad. When are you and dad going to stop being mad at each other? Everyone that is in my class has their mommy and daddy, why do I have to be different?"

"You are not different Oscar, and your dad doesn't want to be in our lives. He has another family and other children. We spend time together every night before you go to bed and we will continue to go get ice cream on Saturdays."

Upset about his mother's response, Oscar stirred his food around on his plate, wishing that Superman would visit him and save him from his unnormal life. Unfortunately, there were a lot of children who live in a broken home. Oscar didn't understand that his dad didn't dislike him, but his dad didn't love Oscar's mother. They had Oscar out of lust and they didn't plan on having a child. After a few years, Oscar's dad started seeing other women and over time he was gone forever. Oscar's mother was going through a period of depression, and her therapy was hanging out with her girls and drinking.

Does it matter who was being the most irresponsible? Does it matter who was right or who was wrong? No. What matters is that Oscar is suffering at the hands of his parents because they are too blinded by pride. If you are reading this, please don't let the children of this world suffer at the hands of parents who do not see the worth in providing a cultivating relationship for their child. If you are the parent who may be in a similar situation as Oscar's parents, please don't let your pride keep you from giving your child the best young life they can have.

Motherless Child Poem

Look at this child…poor child. Where is his mother? Where is his father? Why is he all alone?! Can someone tell me why this child is ranting and screaming with no one to save him?! (backstory about the puddle) The puddle of water seems to be the only one there. He stares at his reflection and notices a host of angels flying above him. He giggles for a moment and forgets that he is all alone.

"Mom, where are you!" he cries out.

Meanwhile, laughter echoes in the house from his mother and some man.

He looks through the windowpane and is struck with a slight pain in his heart. He grabs the left side of his chest and frowns because there is no evidence that his heart had been broken. He starts choking as he reaches towards the angels he saw earlier but is only embraced by the sun as it glows upon his face. He reaches towards the window, as if he could grab his mother's attention, but his mother is a little occupied.

I would hate to imagine his daddy walking by, unable to notice the struggle his son is going through! "Mom!" he exclaims. Too bad mom is only hearing the words of another, as the man whispers into her ear. "Mom!" he cries out. "Why is it that no one cares?"

All he wanted was his mother's love and his father's acceptance. He died from a broken heart and was welcomed by God and the holy angels. He asked God a question.

"Why didn't my mom hear my cry?"

God responded, "Your mom is too busy pushing back her tears and drowning out her own cry that she forgot to listen to yours. Mom has been used by men. Mom looks at her enemies to where she forgets to see her friends. You see, I placed you into this world to bring joy into your mother's life. She was too focused on her own dreams of being some man's wife."

The boy looked down from heaven into the home where his mother sat with the man, still forgetting to check on her son who had died from a broken heart.

My friends, am I setting the stage.

Persistence

I understand that you can't feel your feet because the journey hasn't been nice to you. You feel defeated. You feel like throwing in the towel and surrendering because this pain is too much to bear. Why is it important that you come out on top of your situation?

I want to tell you this while I have your attention. You have a purpose, and there is a reason why you were born. There is a reason why you have triumphed over situations that were meant to keep you down for the count. You are victorious. You are not and have never been defeated. Can you promise me that you'll keep trying? Will you persevere through the thick and thin parts of life? Will you win? The choice is yours.

Prison Tale

Come, walk with me into this place. This is the prison system. Let's walk through the gates that are chained with stained metal. Barbwires caress the surface of each fence. Fully armed guards walk the yard only for their defense. Open the cells, and I will tell you a story.

You see him dressed in the orange jump suit? Him over there. Never mind us choosing one man, look at all of them! Their faces, some filled with hope because their time is almost up.

That guy over there, sitting on his bunk fighting back tears because no one cared that he never had the chance to be a "Good Boy." He didn't know what being a man was supposed to be like. He tried so many times to do things right, while every mistake he made was brought into the spotlight. His lips quiver, shaking as if he was being born on ice. You want to know his story?

Well, he was fourteen years old when he gave up on life. Music, rap music, that was the key to his paradise. It seemed like every song about struggle, sex, drugs, independence, murder, and lies spoke to him like a father. He created a nickname for himself to escape the life he lived. He married the streets and divorced his past. He started selling dope, and that's where he learned his math.

One night long ago, before he came to know this place, he decided to take a long walk to figure things out for his life. It was cold and dark; the streets were empty as the moon casted a shadow against the pavement. Two men approached him without the intent of pleasant greetings.

"Yo man…. Empty your pockets!"

He reached into his pocket to give them his wallet and anxiety took over; as anger and rage filled his heart, he started seeing red.

Pow! Pow!

Two shots, two men dropped as he remained standing. He stood there for a moment as his heart begun to beat fast and his hands begun to shake. He felt a slight pinch turn into a great pain as he grabbed his side. He pulled his hand from the pain and realized that his second shot was an echo of the other man's gun.

Three men laid on the street corner that night. Two men were buried days later and this one… The guy here in the jail cell survived the gun wound. He has been here for fifteen years and has little desire to glance at a clock and no desire to mark a calendar.

That one night for him started many years ago, sometime around birth. Some time when his family could have paid more attention to his accomplishments and his worth. His friends could have been there while he was being picked on because of his Payless shoes and Walmart jeans. His boys could have encouraged him to strive for success and to master a skill. Instead, they gave him a fake identity and called it being real.

Let's go! I am done with this place that is infested with men who had great potential, yet no one cared to show them what it meant to be a man.

The Inmate

Tomorrow sounds like today, and the clock seems like it no longer ticks forward. Forward, his mind couldn't seem to move forward because he was spending his life in a system in bondage. Confined by four walls and metal bars, the sound of inmates flow throughout the prison. It is here, where they receive punishment for their crimes and some stood in lines waiting to call home. Home, a place where most of the inmates will not visit again. Fear creeps inside of the young inmate's heart not sure when freedom will show its face again. Can an innocent person serve time for a crime they never committed? Will they ever see the light of day again? Some are here because they were the same skin color and height as the person who committed the crime.

Junior, a young man from Norfolk, Virginia was transferred to a prison far from home in California. He had just graduated from high school and was going to school on a full ride scholarship because of his excellence in academics. Junior played football and basketball, one of the top players in his region and would soon be living the dream. Well, the dream that he assumed was his was soon taken away from him, which transformed into a nightmare.

"Ma! Roderick wants me to ride with him to South Carolina to check out some school down there. Is it cool?"

"I thought you were planning on getting a job before the semester started? Are your priorities in order? We can't afford to lose an opportunity like this. Your father and I don't have the money to pay for college, so this is something you need to take seriously."

"Yes ma'am! I have my priorities in order. Mr. Scott said that I could work with him at his shop when I get back. I spoke with him yesterday and wanted to be sure before I spoke to you."

His mother trusted him and was aware that he worked really hard his senior year of high school, so she figured it would be a good idea for him to take a road trip with his best friend Roderick.

"Okay," his mother responded. "Don't get into any trouble mixing up with the wrong people while you are down there. Remember what we discussed about priorities."

Filled with joy, Junior started packing as he dialed Roderick's number in his phone.

"Aye bro, what's up! Ma said I was good to go, you packed yet?"

"Man, you know I'm ready. Are you ready? I'm trying to turn up while we are down there. They got some nice looking shorties in South Carolina, and you are the bait to my hook! Don't go down there acting all scared. I'm counting on you," Roderick said while giggling like a high school girl on the phone.

As Junior shoved his last outfit into his gym bag he laughed and responded, "Man, I was born ready. I'm Denzel and you are that white dude from Training Day."

"Alright bro, whatever you say," Roderick said sarcastically.

Less than ten minutes later, Roderick pulled into the driveway with his music blasting, honking the horn in his all black Mercedes his parents got him for his graduation gift. Roderick's parents were both doctors and could afford to get him a brand-new car; Junior wasn't as fortunate. He still drove his dad's pickup truck whenever he wanted to go places.

"I'm out Ma! I love you." Junior ran to his mother and kissed her on the right side of her face.

"Come back here boy and give me a hug, you know I love you right?" his mother said with worry in her heart.

At this time, young black men were getting gunned down by police and by other young black men. She lost her oldest son a few years ago to gun violence, and couldn't bear to go through the same with Junior.

"Yes ma, I know you love me, and I love you too. Tell pops that I'll see him when I get back, and I'm sorry that I missed him. I'll shoot you and pops a text when we get to our hotel."

Junior ran out the front door yelling, "Turn that music down bro! My mom don't want to hear all of that. You are disturbing the peace."

Cries for Peace

You know that this life is passing by; there's no need to pacify the cries of ancestors as we live to die. I am talking about these unanswered bullet wounds from goons, who terrorize our people based on the color of someone's skin or the colors they rock. I know dead men beat against their casket screaming, "Pass me the rock!" When was the last time you hung your brother or sister from a tree? When was the last time you slung words like whips, splitting skin from meat? I am tired of picking up stray bullets like cotton, and I am tired of reminding people about the history they have forgotten. Look at your hands; blood stained from the lives you've slaughtered by not being bothered by these world star kings and queens who beat on each other for likes through your screen. I saw death dressed in a black suit, combat boots, and a black fitted cap. I asked death a question, "Death, what keeps you up at night?" I had to ask death this question and in a matter of seconds he started confessing; "I stay up at night when the street lights come on. I stay up to catch that depressed young lady who can't seem to find love. I stay up to catch that young man who can't seem to find his way home. I stay up because people are calling my name. I stay up because people don't seem to understand how close to them I am. I see you, for better or worse, I see through you. I see your brokenness, your pain, and your fears; I know that you all come to this fight alone because no one truly cares that you are lost and confused. My name is tattooed on your bones; dive into me and dine in with me. As you continue to mate with hate, foreplay with pain, and trade love for the touch of these stranger things."

The Heart of Destiny

Come further into this world we live in….

Over there! Wait!

Someone stop that girl from pulling the trigger!

Click Click!

That wasn't the sound of a misfire. That was the sound of two bystanders recording the suicide of that young lady with no intent on saving her. Let me rewind this scene for a moment.

Her name was Destiny Pardon, she was 5'10 with long legs and dark brown hair. Destiny was every girl's dream and every man's nightmare. Why? Well, Destiny was beautiful and on the outside she was flawless. Her cup size, hazel eyes, thin waist, thick thighs, and bleach white teeth made her every girl's real-life Barbie. As for the men, hmmm. She never gave into the pressures of sex while dating. She would steal a man's heart, rip it apart, then sign it with a kiss and a message that said, "I'm waiting for marriage."

College came, her beauty was out of the frame per-fect. Her girlfriends seemed to boost her ego as if her heart were beating for compliments. Meanwhile, mommy and daddy slept in separate rooms and hearts were as cold as a tomb. Her pillow was more like a sponge that would absorb the teardrops and her black mascara. Her house felt empty although three people were living inside of it. Destiny would punch her bed and gently tap her head on the headboard; we all know that isn't what it's there for. Each night, she would contemplate swallowing pills because she couldn't deal with her reality. To girls she was perfect and to men she was worth it. No one cared that her soul was blue due to the internal beatings she would give to herself with her many thoughts. Destiny felt low in life so she got high off pot.

Things weren't getting any better for Destiny as time moved forward. One night she was sitting in her room with feelings of being worthless and useless. She thought to herself, "Maybe I should tell my mom and dad how I feel." She opened her door with fear and her anxiety leaped through the roof of her home. She made her way across the cold hardwood floor to the stairs as she gazed at her father and mother who were sitting on the couch. The staircase seemed to tremble as she pressed her way down, and she gently rubbed her fingers across the rail of the stairs. As she reached the bottom she took her cold fingers and pressed them against her face to wipe the tears that came tumbling down her cheeks.

"Dad... Mom... I have something to say."

Her heart began to beat louder as she mustered up words to say to her parents. She was more concerned with her father. He was stern, bitter, and angry. "What is it Destiny?" her mom asked.

Destiny responded saying, "Dad, I think you should ease off of mom."

Her father's face went from a soft look to a stone-cold gaze, as he listened for what she would say next.

"Mom does everything you ask, and she never complains. She's not treated like a human being; you treat her like a puppet with strings."

Her father leaped up as if the couch was on fire.

"Shut up Destiny, and go to your room! I work hard to keep a roof over you and your mother's head. I sweat day in and day out to keep food on the table. I break my back to keep you in school! Shut up!"

Destiny ran up the flight of stairs into her room and slammed the door behind her as she flew onto her bed. Crying hysterically, she clung onto her pillow that knew her so well and regretted her attempt at bringing peace into her home.

The next day Destiny decided to go with her friends to the park. She reached inside of her picnic basket and grabbed her father's gun. Thoughts no longer crossed her mind, chills stopped running down her spine, and life no longer existed in time. She loaded the gun as if it weighed one thousand pounds of memories and she put the cold barrel against her head. Her friends turned to her and gasped for air as if it was their life being taken. "Destiny! No!" Click, Click!

Two girls stood across the street with their phones recording for all eyes to see the actions of Destiny. I wish people were more interested in her soul than her beauty and maybe that would have changed her destiny.

Peace

You know, I have dreamed of that "perfect world." Utopia is what they call it. Some say heaven is a fairy tale, but I know it will reside here on earth one day. Can we pause for a moment? Can we take a break from anger, jealousy, envy, and racism? Now that we have paused for a moment, here is what I have to say; beauty is in the eye of the beholder.

Love Underground

Come with me, I see a man stumbling out from his home to his car and he made his way downtown to this bar. Walk with me, we need to get close enough to see his pain. His name is Charles Townson and he is a father of two young girls, Sky and Grace. One might say he is a poor reflection of what a man should be like. Don't we all know what it means for a boy to become a man? Those who know Charles would tell you that he is a very passionate man. His wife Sarah died one year ago on this day, and he has been haunted ever since. Sarah was only thirty-two years old when she passed away; she was a very sweet lady who died unexpectedly. May she rest in peace.

Charles battled spiritually with his Christianity and the God of resurrection. He blamed God for his loss because God was supposed to be Sarah's protection. Charles was hurting much more than some could understand as his nights were mixed with liquor and tears. He sat inside of his three-story home, which was surrounded by a white picket fence and beautiful green grass, as he glanced at old photos of his wife. Each moment he spent with the photos were like self-inflicting wounds from a knife that would slowly peel back the layers of his heart. Charles would cry out in the middle of the night as he relived the night of his wife's death on the hospital bed. His cry would shake the walls of his house and the heart of his children as he would cry in his sleep. He would open his eyes and

21

reach across the empty place in his bed and was continuously reminded of his past. Three hundred and sixty-five days and nights had strangled his passion, vision, and personality; who knew that pain could last. He would pray every night that God would take him away in his sleep. Charles couldn't understand that his children felt incomplete and felt the same as he did. They missed their mother.

Dark nights and misery wrapped inside of death's mystery, oh death where is your sting? Charles had family and friends, but they decided to give him his space. The children had friends, but their friends no longer saw their faces. Time and time again Charles would pray without faith. Time and time again he found that his heart had been misplaced. Home was where his heart could be found, but his home was six feet deep within the stomach of the earth. "Let's just let Charles be, let's let him sleep in peace while he's still alive." That's what his friends would say.

Wait! Wait! Charles had way too much to drink today.

"Charles don't get into your car!" the owner of the bar cried out as he slung open the bar's front door.

It was nearly noon and the tune of the birds chirping seemed to increase as he drove away. Ten minutes after Charles pulled into his driveway, sirens from the ambulance ran wild along with the cries of the crowd and his children. Charles wasn't thinking about the trail of pain he carried with him that year. Charles was found in his driveway with a gunshot wound to the heart. Death by suicide that became alive when they buried his wife, his home, his heart.

Memory

I remember the feeling of holding my dead grandmother's hand.

She was gone.

I couldn't feel her presence anymore.

Grandma was no longer with us.

But why can I feel the cold chills rush through her veins?

Why is this feeling still attached to my brain?

The pain of death is not felt by the dead, it is felt by the living.

Those left to figure life out.

Those left living.

Wondering until their departure.

Allen Simmons

Greatness

Greatness is buried deep within your soul
Your greatness will make you whole
Just lose control for a moment
Do what brings you joy for a moment
Live for the moments
I know that life isn't easy
This blood, sweat, and tears journey isn't what you see
on TV
It's a story worth living
Each stride is worth the living
I promise
You'll see your greatness if you keep on living.
You are who the world is waiting for
Make music from your passions and continue to dream
awake forever more
Living your dreams will cause you to dream awake mak-
ing the ceiling your floor
Walk out of your shame and defeat
Never stop never quit repeat
And repeat
Kiss the face of defeat
Set your enemies under your feet
Fight your fear of anxiety and reach the peak of your
peak
This climb will seem steep
But sometimes you must rest your feet
Rest your mind
Rest your spirit

Can I Speak?

Allow your tank to be refilled by the purpose that God
has given you.
Taste and see the plans that God has given you
Tell distractions to bow down
Tell the walls to fall down
Tell yourself to rise now
Rise Now
Rise up
Rise above the naysayers
And discover your true self
Your inner self
The self that tells you it's time to be selfish
That loving yourself isn't easy but
By God it has to be right
Don't spend time having meaningless sleepless nights
Reach new heights
you can no longer slumber
Be your own plumber and unclog the negativity and let
your voice thunder
Roar
You courageous lions
Soar like untamed birds
Let your word be your word
Bind yourself to these words and fly
Fly even though you feel like crawling
Work hard even if you feel like stalling
Let your greatness shine
Blow their minds as you fix your spine upright
Walk upright
Just walk
Left foot
Right foot
And then take flight
Your greatness is buried deep within your soul

Your greatness will make you whole
Just lose control for a moment
Do what brings you joy for a moment
Live for the moments
I assure you
That you will see brighter days in each moment
Life is but moments
So take your moment

Become the greatest you the world has ever seen

In Hiding

A room with walls made from regrets and complex stories about why you are who you are. What are you hiding from? Faces of your enemies whose weapons scarred your soul mount your wall; they have placed your mind in a dark hole that you can't escape from. Hands reach out from the four faces of the wall, the sound of nails scratch the surface of each wall; the sound is so unbearable! Who are you hiding from? There are no windows or doors and there are blood-stains all over the floor, agonizing pain screams loudly from the floor. Darkness surrounds you, death has you in his grasp and there is no one to call out to---No one! Why are you hiding? There's a wooden box in the middle of the floor. You gather your tears and pain as you crawl inside of it like a dog running away from thunder. You squeeze inside because you feel secure in tight spots, replacing the embrace of your father and mother. You hear something flying around the room but it's too dark to tell what it is. It lands on top of the box, and you feel claws against your forehead. It screams the sound of a vulture as its beak spreads apart and it re-gurgitates pieces of your heart. You are reminded that pain has left you heartless. You pull your knees into your chest and bury your face between your legs. Your brain begins to melt inside of your head and death begins to call your name. Depression pushes out from within your hollow frame. The sound of knocking begins as the impact grows louder and louder. Your pain groans louder and louder, your heart beats louder and louder. A voice calls out to you and it gets louder and louder as it chants, "What are you hiding from?" You call out, "I am hiding from me! It is me, it is me, it is me oh Lord standing in the need of prayer. I need someone to pray these dead bones from the valley of death that I am experiencing. It is me, I am hiding from me."

Bombs Bursting

Bombs over Baghdad, boom! Bombs over Afghanistan, boom! How did I get into this? As I reflect over my life, I remember a time when I could not have pictured this. Death, death is everywhere! Wherever there is war, death seems to follow and it is everywhere. Mirror mirror on the wall, who am I after twin towers fall? I am no longer disguised with camouflage desert gear, I am clicking my heels at attention praying for God to take me out of here! These combat scars mark my soul; bullet rounds were shot to part my body from my soul. I just can't recognize who I am. My God, I can't even recognize whose I am! IEDs and RPGs leave my brothers and sisters overseas. Death tornados through the desert valleys; we've lost so many brothers and sisters. Body bags! These dead bodies can't help me. Body bags leave the war and I know one thing for sure: one of those bags had my name on it. Who am I? These wars have us asking questions like who am I, what am I, why am I here? I stand here mesmerized that my body didn't comply when that RPG landed a few feet next to me. My body went somewhere in the air or maybe the blast pushed me against the surface of the earth; I am not sure. I am not sure how I got to this place where my ears are ringing like a smoke detector, my heartbeat singing loudly and slowly fading into a whisper. I am trying to paint this picture because I want you all to see this as if you were standing next to me. Isn't it amazing how by God's amazing grace that you all can stand next to me? Can you see the sweat from my fears? Can you feel the desert wind brush gently through your hair? Can you hear the cries of mothers, sisters, fathers, and brothers echo through the years of war? Can you understand the sound of bullets grazing across the surface of the earth? Can you picture a new me being birthed from sand? You may ask, "How can he believe in a God who made Adam from Eden's sand, yet he was born from the sands of Baghdad and Afghanistan?" I want you to see that I didn't come home the same! I couldn't gather the pieces of my brain, the thesis to my pain. How could we come home the same? You see, I was born four times and born again three times. My first birth came from the womb of my mother, the second time I was born from the womb of Iraq with my heart unattached. The third time was more than a charm from the womb of Afghanistan, the fourth time and the last time I was baptized into God's miraculous plan. I remember! Gun in my hand, pills on my bed while my Bible rested on the nightstand. Paranoia was tip toeing through the hallway of my home. Gun in my mouth and my finger on the trigger, I was knocking on the doors of heaven wondering if anyone was home! Thoughts scrambled through my head, panic attacks became prevalent as I was attempting to blow a hole through my head! I felt like someone was waiting under my bed! I wanted to die quickly before I laid down for the last time, to finally rest my head. I began to think about why I was feeling this way. Why was I paranoid day by day and why did I feel death coming my way? Why was it storming in my head when it was sunny all day? Why am I? Who am I? What am I? How did I become this way? Seven hours of fighting gun to gun with the Taliban, several hours of losing my mind in a fight with the Taliban. Several years had gone by and I was still at war with the Taliban. My home was no longer a home, it was my new war zone. Every time I opened the door to my home, I had my pistol ready. Every time I checked the closet, I held my pistol steady. Every time I looked behind the shower curtains, my mind was always ready. Why? There was no one chasing me, there was no one in there, it was just me and me. I didn't even know myself and the whole time I was fighting wars, I was fighting against me. From sea to shinny sea I've lost pieces of my soul because I had forgotten about me. I forgot the power of prayer! I forgot that my God was there! I had forgotten that He has always cared for me. I was born again, I found my way within, and I lived more days than him. I mean me. We could no longer be more than just friends; I had to distance myself from me. The war veteran with traumatic brain injury and PTSD. PS, this was for me! So that you all can witness and see that you never have to die at the hands of your enemy. My enemy was on the outside and soon became the inner me. No apologies for shouting out Christ who set me free, from me. I finally found me, in Him.

Scars

I remember when I thought having scars were cool.

I wanted a scar on my face to replace the tears that were like a razor blade, violently making its way down my face.

At times I felt misplaced, living in a world where hearts are scarred because they were never treated the right way.

Broken souls were like broken glass that clashed against the surface of the ground, souls burdened to make it to the next round.

This fight in life will leave you scarred or scared.

You might be afraid to wear short sleeves because your scars could mislead those who are not aware of your past and will misjudge your present; so, as they remain present you hide your scars.

The bullet never left the chamber therefore, I don't have a scar on my head to reflect the tears I shed the night I desired to kill myself.

I tried to heal myself, but I was stuck with a scar on my heart and brain as peace begins to sound like rain thrashing against a metal shed.

Instead of covering my scars I will expose them all, only to free myself.

There is beauty in my pain that paints with bitter brushes of life on my bloodstained canvas.

Can I Speak?

You must be in tune with self to know that your scars are like stars, connecting the past self to your present self.

I am amazed by my body's art, I respect my scars that show how enduring I was and how strong I now am.

My scars are like pieces of art.

Allen Simmons

The Beauty of a Dying Rose

They say there's beauty in youth. Or, is our perception of beauty youth-minded?

What if I was to say that beauty never dies? We have grown in age, wisdom, and intelligence; life has truly been good to us. We may have things we don't like about ourselves, but beautiful things don't always look the same. Take the rose, it once was a seed and later it blooms into a gift. It brings smiles upon the faces of lovers or comforts one who has lost a loved one. Something so beautiful can be in a place where no human eyes will see it and still be considered beautiful. When amongst other roses, it is hard to point out which is different than the others. It is difficult for those who never grew their own rose garden, to distinguish between a good rose or a bad rose. It's much easier to notice a rose when it's dying because it stands out from others. I used to throw away a rose when I thought it was no longer beautiful; but now, I have found beauty in a dying rose.

Rise Up

Sometimes life can be a ditch in the road with no speed bump.

It'll let you crash your foot on the gas when we

do what we want

People got problems and at times life sucks

You can be a poor man, I'd rather stack one million books

Knowledge is power so I eat forbidden fruit
Holy ghost got power and it'll catch you out the suit
And tie
Hell is life
If you choose to live
Maybe you'll get eternal life
If you choose to live

Health insurance through the roof
But heaven got eternal life

No pain no gain
What's heaven without the rain
When it pours
I can see heaven dripping from the floorboards

Allen Simmons

Through the floor, I feel my sword as I stand on God's word

I'm 7ft 11 when I stand on God's word

I'm open 7 11 when I see God's word

Everybody hates rejection

Life ejecting it's expecting you to grow wings

Walk on clouds like angels when you hear the word plain

What's heaven and hell if Christ was never slain?

What's Christianity when you not a white man?
What's world hunger when you selling Christ man?

People need the people
So bread come before heaven

Thy kingdom come before heaven

God I know you made man
But do all dogs go to heaven
Cause these cats got 9 lives

How can people detach from you
And you still grant them life?

Or Is it right
To think I think like God

Can I Speak?

To know when he's speaking or man's speaking for
God.

Well God speak to me
Take me to your mighty seat
Should I stand

Did you create human man
Or did human hands create you?

Gave you names like Jesus

I had a hall pass
Until God turned my left
right

Allen Simmons

Fighting Words

You will always remain defeated!
You'll never be great!
You'll never achieve your goals!
You will always fall short!

(Audience)
Silence

(Me)
Those are fighting words!
I will be victorious
I will be great
I will achieve my goals
I will get back up after falling!

(Audience)
Silence

You are just like your daddy
You'll never be better than your mother
You won't live to be a mother
You won't be a great father

Can I Speak?

(Audience)
Silence

I will be greater for my father
I will be better for my mother
I will live to be a mother
I will live to be a father

(Audience)
Silence
Silence
Silence

I am an overcomer
I am the head and not the tail
I am above and not beneath
I am
I will
I can
Move forward to be the best that I can be
For me
For God
For family

(Audience)

Silence

Allen Simmons

Victory

Life

I'm constantly kicking and pushing, can't seem to coast

Defeat is tickling me while I'm running for the post

Cornered

By legions of demons; I'm dreaming while demons try to stop my hail Mary

I'm not Catholic, I'm Christian

Dipped in water but I'm missing

The in zone

I'm in my zone but I can't stop this play action

Got

Juked by life

Wearing my suit and tie

My boots laced high

Battle fatigue with my disguise

Dressed in black trying to map this sweet victory

The mystery can be seen if you look through history

Is it me or am I fighting in a ring getting boxed in

Jab when I see the hook I'm boxing

Building my stage while surrounded by fire

Can I Speak?

Lord take me higher
Give me eagle wings

I'm shadow boxing now because I refuse to leave the ring

Defeated

You can still win after being defeated
Seated
In high places I can feel my nose bleed

The highlight reel is featuring me

I see me

rising after being knocked down

I was knocked down 6 times and got up 7

My offense is off the fence no straddling the line
I'm defending my territory
That's my feature, life and I

I keep getting these boomerang hits from life after I hit life, somehow I keep hitting myself in the eye.

Self-esteem to the roof but God keeps humbling me

Esteemed to hit the roof but life keeps me stumbling
see

Walk or hurdle
My dreams are fertile
When I lose I'm winning the rabbit defeats the turtle

No matter water
I'll still get a sweet victory

Destiny in a Casket

I found my destiny in basket
Close to a dead man in a casket
I almost passed it
Until I noticed the dead man looked like me

He frowned or smiled like me
I'm pretty sure his silence could speak
Because he had a sound like me
As silence truly speaks
A corpse from the corps of marines
Next to a flag that read Allen Speaks

Well
I felt the urge to hear this dead Allen speak
Under full moons that bleed
I still wore my camo fatigues
I felt so fatigued

Drained from the leeches who needed me, so they
could breathe as I seemed to bleed
I felt life!

and certainly
This moment was like no other

My serenity,
or could it be I'm tripping see

When I found my lifeless body that was when I found
me.

I found that I was better alive than dead
My mission wasn't to stack bread, it was to make heads
lift up at the sign of hope
I am

That shooting star passing through time
To lift the broken mind
To shift the broken through time
To remind people like me that they have a purpose as
we have time

Time to get mines
It's time to get minds
To elevate
Celebrate
the victories
Under the mystery
Of how or why we are still breathing
After all the hell that we've been through
The pain we've lived through
The hopeless times in which we couldn't see through

Chains seemed to be linked from ankles to grave

Can I Speak?

Pain seems to be linked from the cradle to the grave

But hope
Hope is the chain breaker
Hope is the name maker

When you have hope
It doesn't matter
Because you can attach yourself to the way maker

The pain taker
If misery keeps you in an ice box
He can be your ice breaker
With your ski scrapper dreams
Believe that you can break the wind with your hope
As we become wind breakers

Making a sound as we swish our way through life
Bind ourselves to a life worth living
Life is worth living

I, like John Q, saw life at the end
My sun wasn't meant to die
And I was going to live by any means because I didn't
get the q.

Don't wait until you die to find your purpose or desire
to start living

While you still have breath, you have to find your purpose every moment as you keep living

We must find our purpose.
What's your purpose?
Why are you living?
Or what are you living for?

I found my destiny in basket
Close to a dead man in a casket
I almost passed it
Until I noticed the dead man looked like me

Regurgitated Words

Can someone get this thing out of my mind!

Can someone take this sound out of my mind!

Can someone understand this rage that's buried deep
within my mind!

Maybe not.

I just want to vomit out words because I can't process
them properly.

Like uhh

You think it's easy being me!

PTSD from this TBI.

words get stuck on my tongue

until they water my eyes

because I

I am trying to be normal

I am trying to wear a smile

I am trying to exist in society

But all the while

Junior? Let me tell you what I see

I see pride

I see power

I see a bad...

No
I hear gunshots
I see death
I hear
RPGs and screams

I feel my heart jumping from my mouth
I feel my hands shaking like in Afghanistan, my stomach dropping to my knees
Some call their anxiety butterflies but mine stings like bees

My pain
like honey
is now dripping from my veins

Blood
sweat and tears
Blood
sweat and tears

I'm stuck with this feeling of anger because the danger I feel continues to spill over in my mind with fear

I try to fast forward, but each button continues to rewind to back there

Can I Speak?

Rewind to the pain
Rewind to the hurt
Rewind to the gunshots
Rewind until I taste the dirt
Rewind to the smell of gun smoke
Rewind to the sound of explosions

I am trying to digest my words
My life
My purpose
My future
My destiny.

My destiny!
I just want to vomit out words because I can't process
them properly.

You think it's easy being me.

You see the smile
You hear me speak
But I'm still hearing the sound
Of my marines' feet
Fighting hard to remain alive
Into another desert night

So, I...
I'm here.

Trying to digest the words that continue to spill from
my mouth like vomit.

I'm so sick of this trauma
I'm so tired of this drama scene

I need some Dramamine
For the emotional motions of dead bodies surrounding
me like the ocean.

Seen by me and only me
As I regurgitate my pain and
Consume it before anyone notices me.
Broken
Torn
Anxiety is born
So words continue to spill from my brain.
As I regurgitate the pain.

Lead

Even when I'm broken I have to lead
Even when I am without words I have to lead

Hope and purpose are at my finger's tip
I'm pointing straight ahead with my finger's tip.
With hope to inspire someone to transpire in the fire of
life

Leaders are for hire but
most desire to follow
Hope is a hard thing to swallow
Misery loves our company so let's wallow
Hallow

Hallow bodies
Hallow mind
Hallow leaders can be found without a spine
I am connected to the vine
my connection gets stronger through time

You can't lead the blind if you are blind to self
You can't stay blind if you mind yourself

To be a leader you have to choose others
right after you choose yourself.

Irony
It's time to see that being a leader starts by leading

yourself
It's hard to motivate others when you have no value in
yourself
One's self
Could be the reason one can't inspire the mass because
of one's self.

Teach
Teach whatever you are passionate about
Shout in the streets of uptown Charlotte and tell the
city all about
Your
Ability to overcome the jaws of sharks and the cunning
ways of snakes
Teach
Teach about the breach in your relationships
And how ships sink when they collide with other ships.
Good ships, wood ships never stand a chance
If you got money in your pocket then you don't need to
dance
Time on your hand, you have to watch your wrist
The hour hand never stops when seconds turn around
the wrist
Watch
Watch how time moves when you enjoy life
You can't run in the kitchen when you carry a knife
You must love your sister's before you can love your
wife
Destruction is an eruption when you lose focus on life
Depression is a murderer but you can survive
The eagle is the one whose eyes pierce the sky
Have eagle dreams like an eagles vision
But know birds can hit trees when they lose their vision

Can I Speak?

I'm learning lessons, losing lesser like lions licking its
oppressors
I got a taste for victory
vengeance rarely views my mind
I'm winning all the time, even when I'm losing
Less
On the day I lose, I admit I'm losing
We have to take the scars with the emotions that dam-
age the walls of our mind
Change time by reinforcing your mind
Divorcing your zodiac sign
Because
the horror scopes me
To be a libra and says I must have balance
my balance is uneven
Even when I'm learning lessons I'll still keep leading

Allen Simmons

Victorious

It isn't over; this is just the beginning
Open your eyes to this brand new day
New life, new air, a new reason to rise up
Open your eyes to this brand new day

Lift up your head, poke out your chest, and march forward
Let your stride be that of purpose
Let your eyes look to the hills from which cometh your
help and keep marching

I know there's been so much pain
I know some have tried to bring your life to an end
I know that your scars remind you of your past
But know this isn't the end

I see Daniel's rising from the lion's den
I see Joseph's rising from betrayal
I see hope arising from within

Can you see it!
Can you hear the sound of chains falling
From the wrist of those enslaved by sin
I see giants falling from the rocks of women and men

Can I Speak?

Who know and understand that this isn't the end

Rise up and open your eyes to this brand-new day
Let your joy liberate you from your sorrows

Let your feet flee from the wicked who tried to devour
Your peace, your hope, your purpose, your worth
We are all overcomers

Can you see it!
Can you hear the Lord's voice in the air
His power resurrecting the dead, the molested, the outcast and the broken hearted
Rise up!

Son of man
Can these bones ever live again?
My friends, God is calling your bones to live again
Can you hear it!

The sound of God's people shaking the earth
The sound of a woman regaining her worth
The sound of a man establishing his worth

I can hear it!
I can see it!

Oh death where is your sting

Allen Simmons

Oh sorrow where is your stain

There's no time to look back
There's no time to stay back
For God has liberated His people

Christ has brought salvation to His people
We must all rise up

Rise from the ashes of your past
Rise and open your eyes to this brand-new day

War

War!
Imagine being in your home lying in bed, stretching
your arms and legs and suddenly.

Suddenly you hear black hawks and c130s flying over-
head.
All in a moment debris drops onto your bed and your
brain rattles inside of your head and then gunshots.

Gunshots followed by shouts and screams.
You pinch yourself to see if this was but a dream and
again,
you hear screams coming from your mother and father.

You have nothing to protect yourself with and foot-
steps from an enemy you had never met come racing
towards your door.

You hit the floor and slide under your bed as the dust
from your floorboard drifts into your nostrils and you
have to fight away your sneeze.

If you sneeze, you might die.
If you cry, you might die.
If you fight, you might die.

Soldiers with the blood of your mother and father grab
ahold of your dresser and throw it to the floor.

You see the handprint of blood and your mother's
scent floods into your nostrils behind the dust.

Your heart seems to burst as fear grabs ahold of your
soul because you know that you are seconds away from
meeting your maker.

You begin to pray and say to yourself, "if I stay silent
they won't find me."

Tears seem to drop from your eyes as you place your
right hand over your mouth to stifle the sound of fear
as it attempts to leap forward to the soldier's feet.

Their language is foreign, but you can hear the sound of
anger, these strangers are not the ones in danger, they
wanted to find you.

Your father,

bleeding from his stomach, crawls his way into your
room.

He suddenly feels relieved to see that you could have a
chance to be free when he sees you under the bed as he
fights hard to breathe.

Can I Speak?

You make eye contact with your father and suddenly
the soldiers shoot another round into his skull.

Your stomach begins to fold several times and your
mind into several lines as your life flashes before your
eyes.

In a rush to go to the next house, the soldiers never
check under the bed.

That's where the old you can be found, under your bed.

Now you're left with the screams of your mother and
father dancing within your head.

This is what war sounds like from the mouth of its survivors.

It sounds like death...

Not that Hollywood death where the actors are taking
photos after a photoshoot.

War ends when the bodies of enemies lay silent and
their family suddenly has an enemy and it's you.

I mean me.

Someone lost a loved one and it's because of people
like me.

Allen Simmons

Notebook Love

Notebook notebook, open your lips for the tip of my
tongue to French kiss your lines

Let's turn wounded sheep to lions

Open your mouth let me blow your mind

I love how your spine is strong

Let me liberate the blind so they can see these words
are strong

Taste the ink of my pen as I press my emotions into
you

Help me write my mind

Right my wrongs

Help me write these songs

Unwritten

There's something about your blank stare

There's something about the way you stare into my soul
as you steer my broken soul

You make my broken pieces whole

I seem to lose control when I hold you

Let me unfold you

To show you the world from my minds view

Can I Speak?

When I visit you, you allow me to breathe words into
you
I'm so into you I can see myself

I've been cutting myself with papers cuts
I can't contain myself when my papers tough

So tough it could harbor my pain as I spill out my brain
onto its surface

I never knew what emotions would surface
The waves of life make me surf
face, gliding across the earth's face as my troubles, joy,
and pain create massive waves

It's hard to wave goodbye
It's hard for a poet to tell their notebook goodbye

It's hard for a poet to fly when their words are trapped
in a cage
It's hard for a poet to die for when they speak their
poetry is birthed from the stage

Hear me roar!
A lion's heart I cannot part
from writing the dark parts of my thoughts
I'd be lying if my words had never part
From my mind, my soul, my spirit
I can hear it

I can hear it
Words influencing other spirits
You need top secret clearance
If you ever wanted to open my notebook

When I write at times
I'm walking a line
A tight rope
My life's notes
Of pain
From my traumatic brain
I'm an insane terrorist
Strapping my words onto my chest like a suicide bomb-
er
Going into the crowd
Screaming out loud
It's a bomb!!!!
No!!!!

This is poetry.

Grandfather

My grandfather would use his hands to bring life to
seeds just to feed his family.

I had to ask myself if my hands were bringing life to my
own seeds

Or if my hands were working until they began to bleed

But it seems that I've been too busy thinking of trees
that I didn't put in much work in planting seeds.

Questions.

How can one produce fruit if he or she lacks seeds?

Or how can seeds grow when planted by weeds, surely
it'll be choked before it enjoys daylight.

Many choose to work in daylight to be seen but midnight is where dreams grow roots

If you choose to aim for the stars and shoot pass to the
galaxies.

I'm planting seeds that will take me to the galaxy

To grow higher than what eyes can see, I'm planting
seeds.

Those who spend years collecting fruit forget to sow seeds that will give them fruit, like leeches they cling on to others' fruit.

Yes.

They cling on to the fruits of seeds that were planted before they arose to breathe that new air breath in the morning time.

We fear that famine will come and destroy the crops that we never planted.

Freedom is a seed that was planted

Love is a seed that was planted

But how can we enjoy the fruits of those who labored if we never invested time in planting those same seeds of freedom and love?

Like a child with their first baseball glove

People stand in the field of dreams waiting to catch something they can't even see.

Why wait when you never planted your seeds

Why hope for something you weren't willing to bleed

For.

For it is a matter of time before some of these cats reach their 9 lives and soon die before ever planting any seeds.

But first you must believe

That what you reap has to come from your own seeds.

Chains

Chains won't keep me in bondage
Chains won't keep me in bondage
Chains won't keep me in bondage
I will soon be free.

Dark path
Dark night
Dark pain
No light
Dark thoughts
Dark hurt
My pain
My worth!

I'm

on this road and it's yellow with bricks and thorns. I'm
torn like paper. I'm worn like tires from a long journey.
I'm seeking something.

I'm feeling like a slave imprisoned by masters whose
rage dismayed my path to freedom.

Freedom.

I just want to be free
but I
don't know if someone is looking for me.

I see trees
bent over this road
The storms have taken their toll
And leaves are the only thing I see
And they are so lifeless I
don't see any green
In this pasture.

I'm hoping to be redeemed by a rapture
A new chapter
The pain I feel is causing a great disaster inside of my
head.

My head.
I'm bleeding from my head to my toes
As
I froze
on this road that is yellow with bricks
My nose seems to be runny
As tears become an outfit soaked and wet like I'm
swimming in the sea

I began to run

see.
I can see the light.
I can see something that is bright

is it coming my way?

I have to continue to make my way down this road

but I'm so tired.

Heart in pain
it's like fire
being wrapped around my bones.
I just want to go home.

E.T. I just want to phone home

I'm all alone
nothing new appears on this road.
It seems to never end as I grow old
I just want to be free

But this pain is deep within
I just want to be me and descend.

Descend
Into dancing on a path of trees that are green
Next to a river whose

Allen Simmons

Streams take me further into a dream
Of being redeemed.

Lightning begins to strike all around me
This nightmare seems to devour me

Mud on my face like tiger stripes
Fear seems to be all around me and the reason I can't
sleep at night.

Can someone please rescue me?

Clear this path I'm running on
Tear this pain apart from my bones
Surely soon I'll be close to home

But will I ever be free?

Maybe it's time that I should redeem me.
Me
I need to be set free from me

And exchange this torment I've given myself
For a moment to live as myself
Forgiving myself because

I just want to be free.

Can I Speak?

Can someone pay this price for me?
Can someone lay down their life for me?

I can't do this on my own . . .

I hear the chains breaking from my ankles
But does this mean that I'll soon be free?

some would say that the price can never be paid.
I soon stopped running and on the ground I laid.
Surrounded by dead leaves along
a yellow road with bricks.

I grabbed the sticks from the broken trees
That somehow resembled me.

Broken with the debris from my life
Laying on this road for a night
But soon I'll be free.

I'm only me but for now
I just want to be free.

All along this path was created for me
To see
That I truly deserve
to be free.

Allen Simmons

Bottled human

Rage. Anger. Patience. Laughter. Joy. Hope. Despair.
Confusion. Sanity. Love. Hate. Violence, peace, bold-
ness and fear.

See, I'm human too!
I'm holding all of this inside of me too!

This is all of me.
It's hard to explain all of me
When I can only give you parts of me.

Especially since half of you got mouths for ears
Aren't you tired of wasting air?

I get tired of talking sometimes.
It may be hard to believe but I carry heavy weight on
my mind.

I think about death a lot.
Sometimes I think about getting robbed or someone
breaking into my home.
I know I'm not superman but sometimes I love the
smell of harm, especially when it feels like fear.

Can I Speak?

Danger
Danger
Has never been a stranger, I can still feel the rifle vibrate from my anger.
The strain of the trigger as I flexed my finger.

I can still smell the ground burning from explosions
I can smell death in a garden of roses.

I can taste my rage and feel it rattle my cage
Unwrap my face, exposing the veins that dance on my face

This PTSD is something I can't explain
Sometimes I want to hit the desert and spill brains

Lift my pinky in the air to see which way the air is moving to put bullet to brain.

I'm afraid of me sometimes
This PTSD gets the best of my mind
I try so hard to remain distant.

Distant from my past self
Or am I still him?
Is he still me?

Dark thoughts are like sweet music to my ears

Or better yet poetry.

I'm supposed to be talking to get snaps.
I couldn't come up with anything better
Because I'm ready to snap.

This is therapy.

To unpack this weight I'm carrying
I've learned to be responsible about the weight I'm carrying.

That sounds good . . .
The weight I'm carrying . . .

I could never expect for you all to understand how my soul, fragmented and full of holes,
Has been tormented by the terrors of the night.

I still hear cries at night.
I still see fear at night.
Maybe the anger we feel comes from the fear of us not knowing us.
Us not trusting us
With all of our pain.
All of the tears like rain . . .
Collected from the tears of our past.

It's hard to run from your past.

Can I Speak?

The same person keeps resurrecting in the mirror.

Allen Simmons

Silence of a Fall

The silent fall seems to have a sound when it drops
from the clouds

This H2O seems to shower down on the just and the
proud

I took my stand in the rain

Fought back tears because of the rain

I shook the water off of my clothes as I walked through
the door

I could hear the drops caress the floor

Who knew sorrow could find its way through closed
doors?

I am but a door

Aren't we all?

The master's key unlocks what's deep

Overtime we celebrate times like birthdays, anniver-
saries, and funerals

Funerals, that's where we see time stop ticking and the
tock in a dead man's watch fades away in the depths of
the earth

Through time we see people rise to the top of society
just to fall in time for a silent sleep

Can I Speak?

Goodnight, screams the mother to her child

Only to find that child panting in his sleep because his dreams are the nightmares of his week

The week that's filled with weak moments that spill over into one night. Who says tonight isn't our last night?

Pills scattered all over the floor

Nothing seems to silence the heartache of his mother's pain and has left her spirit sore

She takes one pill after the other; each one kills her instincts of being a mother

This mother tried to mask her pain with medicine and now her son will never see her again

Good night

Weight of the World

One early morning the sun appeared in the sky.

It wore bright yellow robes with a hint of gold around its face.

It spoke to me that morning.

With curiosity she said,

"How do you do it? How do you rise with a smile, a smile the size of the galaxy when the entire world is leaning on you?

How can you stand with your feet bruised from your past and your heart scarred by the lips of those you love?

How can you still love?

How do you change the thermostat of your heart and still feel comfortable inside?

Can you see that the world is crumbling from within, yet you choose to go within the belly of the beast every morning; don't you feel tired?

Don't you feel like giving up?

Don't you feel like you've had enough?

Why do you keep coming back up for air?

Isn't it more pleasing to stay in bed with your head against your pillow as the world continues to turn on an axel that keeps you unbalanced?"

I took a moment to reflect on the sun's questions as her light began to pierce through my brokenness.

I agree.

I shouldn't be standing.

I shouldn't be smiling.

I should be concerned and afraid because my shoulders aren't strong enough to bare the weight of the world, let alone my own world.

I should give in or up…

I should stay down for the count.

But how?

I was never trained to put my weapon down for a surrender.

I was never trained to render my weapons of words and ambition down at the feet of some obstacle that doesn't want me to rise above my trials.

For a while

I really considered giving up.

I considered throwing in the towel after raising the white flag, but my flag has been tucked away for some years.

I put it in some place for hopes that I'll never find it again.

So what happens when you lose your flag to surrender?

What happens when you can't take any more and the weight continues to pound on your shoulders.

I refuse to back down.

If my shoulders weren't made to carry the weight of my purpose, then I will die with the weight of my purpose crushing my bones.

I'll stand with my chest towards the sky and my chin in the hands of God, I'll walk proud.

I am proud to say,

I won't give up.

Never Stop
Never Quit
Repeat.

I speak this over my life when my walls don't fall like Jericho.

My hope is that you will continue to march around your wall
Making a sound that shakes the wall and makes the wall
Crumble at your feet.

You and I were made to carry the weight of the world.
We were made to do it together.

Rise

Sometimes we lose sight of who we are while still finding out who we truly are. We are like broken vessels whose ships sink below shallow waters and river banks.

It's no wonder people can see our mass as we lay on the floor of this riverbed to think.

We attempted to scream because of frustration as the cold river water flowed through our lungs.

Did you notice?

Did you notice that we could stand, and our heads would be above the water's surface.

We are too consumed by our pain so we stay beneath the surface.

The sun's rays pierce through the water, as the cold sand seems to burn our feet like frostbite.

No creatures are swimming around because of our toxic nature, our heart is torn into two forming a crossbite.

Why is it that we are choosing to drown when we could just stand in waters that only consume us when we lay down?

Why can't we walk to the shore in the midst of this
moment with the sun to our crown?

Caps and gowns await us on the land.
Capture the ground with our feet, as we march forward
to land.

We will rise.
Rise for the future.
Rise for the moment of truth.

The truth is that we are only at the bottom of this shallow river because we are choosing not to stand; it is not
because our ship wrecked in shallow waters.

Art

Art.
Poetic art
Human bodies are like poetic art.
Models.
Bending at the limb to get the eye behind the camera to
focus as she remains focused.
Holding breath and thought
This human body becomes art

Twisting neck
head slightly bent
Back like the letter C,
her eyes piercing through my soul from the cover of
this magazine.
Her arms outstretched, fingers spread against this wall
that is deep dark and blue like the ocean.
It's almost as if she is leaning on water
Putting all of her trust in her bended knees.
There's no sign of squeeze or strain
She's graciously presenting her body as art.
Maybe
just maybe
she's falling, and her fall was the perfect picture for the
world to see.
Maybe just maybe she's struggling to keep her back fully
bent,
Sometimes art makes you bend over backwards to see
life from a different perspective.

With art you can't be too selective
You can't search for art like a detective
It is usually right in front of you.
It usually looks like you.
You can be like her.
Or maybe you are like her
Fighting to remain in position so that the world will see
you in some highlife position
But to me our pose can seem kind of awkward.
Posing to be standing when we are supposed to be fall-
ing
We are supposed to be on our back but somehow we
forced it to bend
We, like her, show no sign of stress but I know within
This position isn't comfortable.
Art
Poetic art
Human bodies are pieces of art
In pieces we become God's greatest masterpiece.
Our brokenness can be quickly fixed. Like a portrait
framed with bronze or gold and sometimes plas-
tic. Our covering glass may shatter when the world or
some girl or boy drops us on our face, but we will be
okay.
We'll be okay because our frame is not the art,
the soul is the vibrant work of art and being poetically
correct just means you're speaking your truth.
Your truth is that you're supposed to be true to you.
Your pose is art too.
Just like the model in this magazine, your pose is all
they will see for a moment. Even if you're seen on a
billboard.
So let your pose be you,
However twisted your life may be

Can I Speak?

It is art
Poetic art
And art is beautiful.

Allen Simmons

Glowing Soul

Soul...
I know you glow

I know your flow

I know you're in there somewhere.

I'm here and you are there.
Tainted but it's clear that we are one in the same.

My frame is the same, but how did you get here?
In there, out here

I'm looking into me, but I can't seem to get out of here

Here, where my rib cage is broken by my heart

Here, where my soul turned holes into pot holes

My damage wasn't as wide as it was before I

was damaged.

Manage
Yourself

You Managed
yourself

Can I Speak?

I searched my inner parts
In order to manage myself...

Myself
I barely recognized myself as I stood in front of the
mirror. .

I leaned closer and pressed my hands against the sink's
shelf

Searching past my eyes to think
Self
Think

To think about the man I couldn't see
I mean, I didn't choose to see me with all of my flaws
I had to think.
Think about the man I desired to see

Why...
Do Your eyes hold so much pain?

That's what I said to me.

Steadily
Gazing through the pain to find a boy who is still in
pain because he doesn't know if his mother really loves
him.

I mean, does he even love his mother
Like he loves his brothers
And other women he called mothers

Others,
Strangers seem to capture the soul of my love instead
of it being my mother's love.

I'm searching for the man who is lost in another galaxy

After while I'll see

I'm still searching for the young man who lost his way
down a drunken path

The aftermath
Was after class

I'm in a session with my inner self

the half of class.

Present

As I stood in the mirror looking into self
I had to dig deep within myself to notice the roaring
lion waiting to break free from his cage

This cage became weightless
Shapeless self, I need you to find your inner rage

I can see the rage as I turn the pages of your mind
I hear you back bend under the night
That fire fight was a fighter's fight.
Gun fight left me sleepless at nights

I see the time when bombs were bursting in the night.

Can I Speak?

The angels could be seen traveling from day into the
midnight.

I see a fight.
I see you fright a little
Thinking your night would turn you into an icicle

Those cold hearts couldn't play fittle
Your heart was pure, but your patience was little.

Church boy but my hands are brutal
Noodle slippery slimy belly full

You don't know your God, his pockets never fold

Parking meter, he paid the fine money never old

I am a believer.
Leave it to beavers to break through trees
The drama mean; it got me sea sick
I never really saw sick or gray hairs until resurrected
from the devil's chair.

Sentenced to death
You resurrect
No scars but brain has been battling death.

Death.
Smelt like burnt souls
Head bleeding from a hurt soul
After war you lost control.

You didn't' know if this fight would end with you laying

on your back with blood spilling from your body,
through cracks of war's wound
You walked up high
straight out of the boxes room.

Oddly you came home and met the odd me
My mind wasn't ready, this is part two.

Walking past the mirror
I began to stand and stare at the man in the mirror.

Asking if war really changed me
God saved my soul, but I couldn't part the sea.

Even when I could still see my greatness shining in the
mirror, I saw my pain blinding me in the mirror.

I thought suicide
Suicide felt like it was the truth inside

Eyes were brown but soul black inside.

I was thinking suicide could rest my mind, I had to test
my mind to see if it could still shine for my third eye to
see.

I see me
With pain
And as I strained
I could see my pain rising up

I feel my soul rising up
I felt in control as I was rising up

Can I Speak?

My reflection

My rejection to self

could be no more
This Is my door
Is
My perfect opportunity.

I am me.
I was he before he became me
Destiny
That's what I said to me
Man in the mirror

I am who I see in the mirror.

Thank you, Sergeant Simmons.

Allen Simmons

Who Are You

I was lost and now I've been found
My soul was twisted in the ground
And for the crowd
I put down my crown

I left my throne with a toothache
Shattered my soul just to live fake
Outside of my identity

I became someone I've never seen before
That man who had to press his ear to his own door

Paranoid

I slowly destroyed my identity
Since 23
I've been that man for far too long

I had to mix up the song
To lift up from the wrong life I was living

I will never be the man that's not me
No gold or chain will change me

It's strange see
We allow the world to paint us in a frame we never
belonged in

Can I Speak?

We became an enemy to self just to gain friends

No more
Heartache and pain from the hurt that came
When people said you wasn't good enough, even when
your blood became their paint

Painting over their scars with your smile
Cleaning their wounds with your love

Allen Simmons

Stand

Lift your head
Stand up tall
Erect your spine
And walk straight
You may drift, but walk straight

Look deep into your mirror and tell me what you see.
Who are you?

That's what I asked myself!

I said

Self are you listening?

I don't know who you are!

Why do you have so many scars?
Why are you trapped inside of those bars?

Are you who you say you are?

Are you still that little boy hurt from being an outcast
to the black class?

Are you that boy watching his friend get hit by a car?

Are you that boy who watched his blood leap from his

Can I Speak?

body?

Are you still you?

Are you still the man who lost his way down that yellow
brick road?

Are you that man who poured his soul with liquor to
destroy the picture of the man in the mirror?

Are you getting nearer to self?
Have you learned to master self?

Are you still you?

Do you have a clue?
Have you allowed yourself to be painted by the world's
idea of who you are?

You are dynamic
You are the me that I need

You are my last breath, you are my last test
I have to master myself

Show myself that I am who I am
By remaining the resurrected me
I was buried deep
Deep in the belly of hell
Yet still I prevailed

Still I rise

Allen Simmons

Ethics

You want me to be just like you, don't you?
No ethics or is it no morals
Are my morals mixed up with my ethics
That my identity is reflecting everything I've been
taught?

You can't teach morals
You can teach ethics.

You can't trick morals
But you can twist ethics.

Like
Did they really mean that working a 9 to 5 is ethically
correct?
You bend your back to turn necks
So the world can see you follow rules.

Some become ethical tools
When they follow rules they don't believe in.
Do you follow the ruler you don't believe in?
Measuring your morality, sexuality becomes a question.
Many question their sexuality because their morality is
mixed with ethical principalities.

I understand..
I may be Christian, but I don't allow my ethics to become a weapon of mass destruction.

Can I Speak?

Destroying my brother or sister for being a person who doesn't fit the picture of what being a man or woman means.

In a world full of labels, we kill dreams.
Before I was labeled, I had other dreams.

Dreams of being an actor
Rapper
Singer
Poet

I didn't know that

My ethical standards
Would hold me to a standard
Where my morals
Weren't ethically right.

I slept around and judged myself
Because sleeping with a woman who isn't your wife was ethically left and not right.

So I was

King of Jezebels
King of sin
King of greed
King of lust
King of lies
King of many hills I wasn't supposed to climb
Because it wasn't ethically right.

It is possible

Allen Simmons

For a person to be morally right
Without feeling ethically wrong
Giving the world a new song.

I'm morally turned on by my mistakes.

I wouldn't be ethically great
Without my morals.
My standards
Seem to shape shift in the cameras.
My identity is my identity by my standards.

The world will not die with me
My passion of Christ will die with me
I know that crooks and thieves are ethically wrong
But sometimes it's important to eat from the forbidden tree
Or you might die.

You might not have a plate to eat on at night
So who am I to question your morals?

Your morals
Create who you are in that moment.
In a moment
A person's morals can be seen in an ethical tree
Of knowledge.

Once you learn who you are, some ethics stick to you
so you pay homage.

Just don't lose respect for yourself
Continue to take your life book off of the shelf

Can I Speak?

And create knowledge as wealth
So you'll never trip on the ethical
Testicles of society.

Fight for your sobriety
Because it's morally right.

Be morally right
Or you'll be ethically wrong.

A poet with a poem of peace
A poet with a poem that will release
You from your inner beast.
The beast that society created
With ethical principles unrelated to you.

Allen Simmons

Imagine That

I know I wasn't designed to drink wine over spoiled
cheese

My failures are over me
I am over the
Late nights filled with lazy eyes that hide behind tears
of confusion because the delusion was ruined

The delusion that I was a filthy marine with blood
stains on my tee
is it me?

Or was I me?

I'm trying to break free from this PTSD, but sadly it'll
always be a part of me

Or am I glad because PTSD has made me

free

Free because
I left me behind with a loaded chamber and pills, loaded more drinks to bottle

Imagine that
You went from bitter to better
You learned to weather the storm

Can I Speak?

You continued to mend your broken heart with the
strength of your own song

I seemed to drink more of that red wine
As my mind continued to define the boarders of anger
and rage all on one stage

On one page I was strong but right then I was weak

I honeysuckled defeat
Yet still I rise
Or rose
I am rising

Like waves from the stormy sea
I see me rising
Thrashing against the obstacles that didn't want me to
be free

Imagine that

Imagine the fact that I am alive because I survived the
war inside of me.

It isn't the war against man that we seek
It is the war within you and me

Imagine that

I was fighting to remain me and assumed I lost myself

But I see within myself

I will continue to rise within

So self

You will always bounce back
You will always grow
You will always become stronger

No wonder

I've bounced back when I was inside of an eggshell of
betrayal and a broken heart

The yoke was made easy
I receive thee

I've grown to smile when it rains

I've become stronger by pain
For pain is weakness leaving the body
Or am I only strong because I became weak in the pain
and used an IV

The source the keeps me living

Imagine that...
All this pain gave me purpose
It feeds me my dopeness
I'm hoping that my right now isn't where I'll be
You have to get set free from the pain and be
Strong and filled with purpose
Imagine that
Your pain still gives you purpose
You have purpose from all those worthless times

Can I Speak?

Time is never worthless as long as you still have breath
in your lungs
You have to go dumb to realize you don't know everything

Imagine that

You don't know everything
You can't shape the world from your bed
You have to lift your legs and jump from the bed to
create your purpose

Allen Simmons

Legend Nipsey

All my life, been grindin' all my life
Sacrificed, hustled, paid the price
Want a slice, got to roll the dice
That's why, all my life, I been grindin' all my life

Light of the darkness
Why are you so afraid?

I am alone,

light within darkness
Surrounded by death

Death surrounds my home
Town
Marathons can bring you to your victory lap

And the dead resurrect like zombies
Thirsting for blood and bodies

Light.

Just a strip of light can keep evil K9's away
Bullets shatter the batter of bones bending backs because bullets break bones.

Flesh and bones leave the dead for the day
Imagine losing wife and child as the soul departs on this

Can I Speak?

day.

Another night
My hunger strikes
Will Smith and Weston
Got me suited for war like a western

These west stars
Running marathons

Child asking mom when is daddy coming home?

Got mothers asking the Father why did you leave us all
alone

Hustle Nipsey hustle
Nipsey hustled for the world.

Can't say I knew of
Nipsey's hustle
But I know the world is reflecting the light of his fame
or flame

Born legend, die a hero
Zero zombies, die a hero

Many men sleep awake
Never woke

but they feed on hate

Trigger squeeze make em famous
Everybody going to hate Chris

Allen Simmons

You kill, you kill, you kill a man
Pray the Lord gets you before Nipsey's fans

I pray the Lord save you
For the sake of Nipsey man

I pray his wife get through the heart break of her
Nipsey man.

I hope none of you die like Nipsey man
I hope your body gets old because of your wisdom.

I pray your hustle gives you a nip of hope.

My hope is that no man will be in Will's legend

I am legend
And you are legend

hopefully we don't have to die because of hate
On our last victory lap.

Emma Goldman

If I can't dance to it, it's not my revolution.

These chains.
These chains are holding me back

These chains got my wrist leaking blood because I have
been fighting for so many years to get out of them.

I hear the universe beating on drums from the pain that
comes when oppression is the lesson we never learn.

I cried tears as my skin started to burn
The more I fought the tighter it got
Oh how my wrist continued to burn

I could feel my stomach turn
Inside out
I'm trying to see this world from the inside out
Outside in
Too many people die from the outside in
Because man
Man has revolted against man
Black man
Finds the tunes from gun shots
In the tomb of the trap
But I can't back it

I'm trapped in these chains with my back against the

wall
I hear violence playing its trumpet aloud
But I can't bow to every blow
I can't let now be the moment my knees bend
And my back buckles

I'm in chains hoping for a revolution that sounds like
me!
I'm beating against the walls of this room praying for
God to set me free
So the world can see

My revolution.
The type of revolution that takes guns from the hands
of a man before he becomes a murder

The type of revolution that brings mothers to tears
because her son isn't another murderer

I can't seem to get anyone else to dance to the beat of
my heart's drum
I can't seem to get their feet to run from anger to peace.

Pride truly comes before the fall.
And pride must be higher than the highest tower because I hear my brothers babbling

About killing

So I guess it's time again for God to confuse our language

I can only use sign language because my words seem to
fall on deaf ears.

Can I Speak?

How can we switch gears and overcome this year?

This year and the rest of the years, I pray that prayer is
the language we speak
And here in this moment we become weak so that God
is made strong.

I'm tired of seeing wrong
I must break free from these chains.
I must break free so brains can exist as the engine that
brings hope in the midst of this division.

How can two walk together less they are yoked
How can two walk together less they agree that hope is
in the same direction.

Our direction needs to change
So these chains can't keep me bound anymore.

Let's not let chains keep us bound any longer
This revolution sounds like thunder
And
If I can't dance to it, it's not my revolution.

So with this

I orchestrate a new song
A new sound in the air.

The time for fruitful revolution is here.
Come near.

Taste and see that this is our moment
Let's start a revolution

Safe

I can't save you!
So let go of the rail, stretch your feet towards the water,
and leap
You don't deserve to live!
You don't deserve to kiss opportunity!
You don't deserve me to give
My life for you, this isn't that opportunity!

You expect me to risk my life when you can't even
stand to fight for your own?
You expect me to sweat over your destiny
When you can't even lift your hands to plow your own
land?
You can't be serious.

You talk so loud when your friends surround you
But under the cover you can't keep a constant group of
friends around you.
Your pillow must smell like
Onions because you wake up complaining and crying
about life not being fair.

You brush your teeth with bitterness
And wash your body in regrets.

You can't seem to lift your neck to move forward because you expect someone to carry you on their back!
Your back must crack every day

Because you continue to bend over backwards because
you're too afraid to fall forward.

I do look forward
To the day when you decide to fight for the things you
ask for.

I pray that you'll awake tomorrow morning with your
pillow smelling like joy and pride
I pray you open your eyes and thank God that you have
another opportunity to chase your dreams with a smile
on your face.

I hope every place you go shines from your impact

I hope you see the back of your purpose
And remain out the backseat hoping for purpose.

I pray you find some kind of purpose.

Because I can't save you.

I'm too busy saving the ones who fight to stay afloat
Who face poverty with a sense of hope
Those who walk when the world has its foot on their
neck
I hope you lift your neck because you finally feel like
living
You finally feel like giving up
Bad habits
The sad theatrics.

I hope you live
I hope you tell me to shut my mouth when I tell you to

Can I Speak?

jump off the next bridge
I hope you choose to live
Tough love don't mean this kid don't got love
I just need you to fight for your own life.

Before you expect me to lay down mine.

Don't worry . . .

After all.

If you decide to stretch your feet towards the water and
let go of the rail.
I'll be sure to haul tail
And sail over the rail just to save you.

Tough love.

Allen Simmons

Freestyle

Day turns to night and night turns to day
They are
Seeking for answers about the world today

I see
black lives
painted like stop signs
I see it, the red dripping down his bones like a freeway

I see Black Panthers hiding way in a distant land

I see the need for a people to build a man with purpose

Life gets hard when you don't know your purpose

Skin color divides the country and that's just the surface

I created the inner me like me so that I can see the enemy

I be the enemy
I being man because that's the enemy

So man beats woman
Woman kills child
A world where Disney World is a special place
Is questionable right?

Can I Speak?

Isn't it odd

That children can't experience Disney World in their
backyard?

Basketball in the courtyard.

Go hard or go home.
Live life
it's your song
No move
that's your wrong
Do right and you'll do no wrong

Black man.
I need to see you rise from bullet wounds and missions
of suicide
You reside
On the same side
But colors kill
That's a suicide.

Be strong.
Be courageous.
Fight for your life.

Allen Simmons

Appearance

Do I look like I'm simple?
I swear I'm not

I got two left feet and I'm walking backwards

some think I'm some fitness coach who motivates
minds to see

All the while I'm this unfit cat constantly motivating the
inner poet in me.

So I speak motivation
I question minds.

I'm the poet shooting shots while your head's in the sky

People ask me why
Do I speak

I tell them my mind and heart are twins, and I'm reaching for peaks.

When my rhymes are weak
I scheme the peak

At times

I don't really know if I'm meek

Can I Speak?

Mills of dollars on my mind and I can't see

So I grab the wind's shield

That's the Spirit of God that keeps my blinds open until the wind chills.

I'm sort of a churchy guy but that don't mean that my mind's not open wide

I'll keep smoking this hookah while you try to figure me out

Riddles and Skittles in Arizona

dead man

Zimmer killing them man till it's hot like hell Arizona

I'm black and I'm proud, no need for co-signing

I am me

The fit mind of a guru
Making concrete minds from noodles

Popping toaster strudels
I'm not asking for clues though
I'm kicking rhymes punching lines like judo.

How many cats like me do you know?
I could act like me

and you wouldn't know.

Allen Simmons

It's blood, sweat, and tears
The type of journeys on which I've traveled

So when I scream Bombs Over Baghdad

Boom

Don't be rattled
I'm wolf to cattle
Grim reaper lets battle
I'm ready

An open book with hidden pages
A ticking bomb on open mic stages

I get courageous
when I see victory making its lap
When I hold trophy in lap

Some long long time from now as an old man

I'll write my story with the last ink in my pen
My script says I'll win

So I'll finish where I began

Forever the guy who speaks poetry

Do I look like I'm simple?
I swear I'm not.

Loyalty

What is loyalty?
Tell me what it looks like.

Does it look like you?
Indeed,
It doesn't look like me.

I can't see it and talk is cheap and I'm rich in self
So I can't paint loyalty all over myself.

Watch the one who claims they are loyal

Didn't
Judas kiss Christ
And
So let's question the hype

Peter denied the Lord

Yet we still want to play the Christ

Play the role of loyalty
So
In the morning

Wash your face before looking in the mirror

You might see someone disloyal while you're staring in

the mirror

Is the mirror getting any clearer?

Satan didn't fall from heaven because he couldn't stand
to be the armor bearer
And he fell from grace

He fell because his loyalty was misplaced
And displaced

The one who first reflected the light of God
Proved that loyalty has no face

I swear no one is loyal

Even I
Disloyal
I denied God before man
Kissed the ring once He showed me His hand
And His plan
Yet still there are days when I ignore His plan

So I stand as I'm seated
Seated as I stand
Showing the hands of jokers at bat
Man
I can see them from the stands.

No, I'm not saying it's you alone
It's me and every person who will die and be buried
alone

So you are not alone

Can I Speak?

My goal is to get you to stop chasing loyalty
Hope for loyalty
Dream of loyalty

Because the same one who dreams has once been disloyal.

So tell me

Who is loyalty?

Allen Simmons

Inevitable

That predestined moment when body no longer has air
to breathe
When tree no longer has leaves that cleave onto its
branches

The moment when the hour hand clicks forward again

Time slips away into the day and soon
The inevitable happens

Death is inevitable
That's why it eats up human lives as if they were edibles

Incredible
It's incredible that we build strong towers and frown
when the fruits of our labor go sour

For now is the hour for power but trust
Death is coming soon

We pretend that we have more hours in our noon to
dance in the sun's light as we bind our minds to love
for the first time

We kiss but soon we will cry
On some cold winter night
Or some warm summer day
It could be our last

Can I Speak?

because death

Death is inevitable
Death never gets a return to sender
When your life is surrendered it does not render grace

So in this place
At this moment
How do you value your time
Can you feel time slipping from your fingers
As you grow old and hopefully wise
You start to understand that time is never on your side.

Time was never on our side
And it takes time to die
It takes time to rise
But everything that rises must fall at some point in time

Time

Whether the clock is ticking or if the clock no longer
runs, time will outlive man
And that's something I don't understand
So God,

How can you make me in your image and likeness when
I can feel the tightness of death around my neck
And the chains of uncertainty gripping at my legs
I beg!

Why am I not fully made in your image!

The image that is outside of time

Allen Simmons

I shattered my mind trying to figure out why I'm so
broken and in my brokenness you proceed to make me
stronger
Even though death is inevitable

Will you all choose to live with such a purpose that
death gets bothered when you surface over your pain
and mistakes?

Will you allow time
The constant ticking of time
To mold you into your greatness

After all
Time and death are inevitable
So now let's live like now is the greatest time

Forward

Do I have something to look forward to?
Failure seems to be eating at my roots.

And

I can't stand failure

I can't stand the way it looked at me as I would stand in front of the mirror

The man in the mirror.

This person did not look like me

No.
His head was too low

And his smile didn't seem to show

At times

I would park
Under a bridge
On a dark road.

I would flip my visor and glance into the eyes whose gaze was fixed on me.

Allen Simmons

I saw hurt.
I saw pain
I saw failure and he knew my name
But I knew my name
Yes...
I know

My name

Who was I?
Am I?
Will I?

I can't seem to remember the days, but I remember the wave.

The wave of failures that brought shark-like bites from fights with my identity.

I could pretend to be me.

For some time I thought I was me

I couldn't see, the soul that was locked

Down by depression's chains

I can feel the chains.
Cold
Heavy
Dry.

Dry.

Can I Speak?

I had no living water pumping through my veins
And chains wasn't the only thing holding me back.

I was stuck in this crack with a stack of hope under-
neath my feet and still

I couldn't see
From out of this crack
I braced my back and pushed from its face

I could taste
Victory.

I found myself rising from death into victory
It's a mystery

That my history isn't finished
My future isn't diminished
My now is my beginning

Right now.
I'm standing
Running like bolt and flash
I'm feeling like a mix of man and super

I spun the barrel and pulled the trigger
The gun clicked every time.
Weapon my mind

I realize my mind

My mind is the very thing that gives me hope
Because everything that kept me low

Is now beneath me.
My hope comes from my past
I made it past my past

So yes

I have something to look forward to.

Darkness

There's this place that I'm afraid to go.
It's dark down there.
There's no light or joy down there.
I hear screams.
I hear bones cracking.
I here jaws smacking together.

I feel the fire touch my skin
I think I made it in
I made it to hell

Oh
How my well has been filled with fire and brimstone.

This is not where I thought I would be.
These thoughts got me in hell tormented by what I've
seen.

I've experienced
My heart racing
Creating spaces in my breathing pattern
I have seen my life flash before my eyes when that RPG
hit close to me.

I was supposed to be
Somewhere sipping gin and juice
I wasn't used to this pain.

Allen Simmons

I couldn't seem to tame the inner me
Next to self I could not see a future for the future me.

I got this war stuck inside of my head
I tried to paint my bed with the picture of me painted
on the bed.

My head hurts
I can't seem to see past me.

Where is this tunnel of light?
Where is this path that lights bright for those who are
coming out of darkness?

I made earth shake when I marched from hell
I watched my hope swell
When demons failed to make my experience
The end of my life experience.

I found my soul in a casket
I almost passed it
Until I noticed me.

Rollercoaster

Anticipation.
Fear.
Anxiety to the roof
Stomach uneasy
Tell me, how do you

Stomach the pain of facing your fears.
You are afraid to travel the path of life's rolling coaster
You supposed to
Be on the ground watching others rise
Yet you rose to the sound of fear
And now you bear witness to your ascension in new
dimensions

You prepare for your ascension
Don't look down as you are rising up
Let life take you up

With expectations, you sober up
Destined for greatness, I hear your chains clinking up
I see you going up
Just don't look down. Trust me

This life will be sure to take you down
But don't look down
Keep your head up

Money has no power unless you understand how to

stack your bread up

You paid for it

This ride ain't free

You are on the verge of being set free into your destiny

Stand next to me
Or rather sit

This life is a rollercoaster
But don't let fear take you over
You are destined for greatness

Waves

I feel the waves thrashing against this boat I'm in
Its force of trouble pushing my boat over, please God
don't let me sink

Don't let my lungs become a vessel for this oceans water
Don't let my eyes become bloodshot red with tears
dripping down my face against the oceans face

Dear God please don't let this ocean overshadow my
face

Turn my sails away from this storm
I'm lifting my arms
I truly surrender
I give myself away

Just don't let this be the day my boat decides to sink

Why is your wind howling aloud?

Is it because I was too proud to beg for mercy?

Cast me not into this sea of torment
Its water is up to my ankles, and I'm beginning to panic

I'm beginning to feel overwhelmed by my situation
There's never time for relaxation

There's a war inside of my boat
Inside of my mind

Am I not worthy of a second chance
I tried to kick H2O but somehow there was

Way too much water to fight

I feel as though this night will take me by storm
I'm in this storm and there's no one searching to rescue
me

There's no lighthouse from what I can see
Oh God just set me free . . .

I'm not free yet

I go down to the lower level of my mind

I tried to fight for my mind but this time

This time I felt too weak to fight this storm
But something inside of me was telling me that I wasn't
born to lose

I wasn't born to die in an isolated ocean with water
overpowering me

Or problems over towering me

I wasn't destined to die In this PTSD
I'm jumping

Can I Speak?

I'm jumping

I'm ready to take this leap of faith
I'm ready to get this gun out of my face
I'm ready to lose this taste

This taste of a bitter battered soul

I'm ready

Shouldn't this storm be over now because I'm ready?
Shouldn't the pain stop because I'm ready?
I'm ready to live!

Why?
Why is death still taunting me and my sails are down in
the midst of this raging ocean of a beast that's stuck
inside

Of me?

Oh it's me . . . It's me
It's me oh lord
Standing in the need of prayer

Prayer

Someone must be praying for my rise
I can hear the sky open and heaven descending down to
earth

I can hear victory bells jamming on the shore!

I see a light at the end of the storm

Allen Simmons

I feel the sun and its warmth
I feel life
And
I feel alive
I feel my soul rising to the sky
And from a bird's eyes you could see it too

I have been down in a valley with my heart attached to
rocks
I have been in the face of death

I have met myself in the face of death

And now

Now I'm dancing until I face death because I chose to
live

I chose to live

I chose to thrive

And now I live my life for the moments

I live my life knowing that in one moment
I can be here today and gone tomorrow
Tomorrow
Tomorrow
Tomorrow has its own worries
Tomorrow has its own cares

So I live in the moments

Resilient

Did you know

To be black in America you must wear your skin inside
out. For people fear darker skin before they fear the
words from your mouth

To be black in America
You must understand that your bones can still crack
under trees

Your forbidden fruit was lust
Hence why

We kill for things

To be black in America
You can't stay out past midnight

You can't play cops and robbers
Because the cops might think you are the robber

To be black
To be black
To be of color

Allen Simmons

It is not my brown skin that should fear you

If this applies to you

My skin should tell you that I am resilient, strong, victorious, and BOLD

My black is BOLD
Beautiful, gold sun kissed

We are not a people of curse
We are a cure to the sickness of this world
Heal us and you'll see how black the world can be

For darkness is not about fear, death, murder, and vanity
Darkness means rest, comfort, and faith

It takes faith to walk out our doors today

And most importantly,
It's still a blessing
To be black in America

Acknowledgements

I would like to thank my amazing wife, Amber, for being supportive and interactive in my writing journey. Thank you for standing with me throughout my journey, my mental breakdowns, my ups, and my downs. I am forever thankful for the love you possess for me. I admire your strength, your resilience, and your gracious spirit. I cannot thank you enough for being who you are and for supporting me the way you do.

To my father and mother, Levi and Brenda Simmons, thank you for believing in me. You both are loving and have always been in my corner. Thank you both for being great parents and working all of these years to ensure that your children were able to live comfortably. I appreciate when I see you in Charlotte, and I am forever thankful when I can visit in Charleston and share laughter and love while watching T.V. I am proud to be your son.

To my sisters Nakia, Renee, and Ebony, you are all the true definition of beauty. I've seen you all rise when the odds were against you. I've seen you all love your children and protect them with all your power. I am inspired by you all and am proud to be your brother.

To my brothers Emanuel, Bryan, and Shane, I know that time and distance has had their way with us, but it can never take away the bond of brothers. You guys have continued to live in a world where it is difficult to be a black man and yet you all prevail. Bryan and Shane, continue to be great fathers and know that you can do whatever you put your mind to it. Emanuel, I appreciate your love and concern for family. I know we haven't spent a lot of time together but know that I value you. I enjoyed spending time with you in Atlanta when Amber and I were in the area. I pray you all continue to rise.

To the rest of my family, friends, Superfriends - big ups to A Poet Named Superman, Revive Church, Brownsville Community Church of God, Red@28th, Dubose Middle School teachers, Summerville High School teachers and coaches, CBMC -Bill Montross, Warrior Scholar Project, Notre Dame Staff, Reboot Combat Recovery- Matt Thomas thanks for the gas lol, yes my car ran out of gas. Mandy McCaslan at UNC Charlotte, thank you for being there when I was close to the edge and wanting to give up in my pursuit of my degree. You are selfless and a blessing. Good luck in your future endeavors.

Luke Mulvaney, I couldn't have finished this process without you. You are one of the best salesmen I know; you are great at your craft and I know that you will go far. Thanks for supporting me at my events and in my pursuit of being a speaker and author. I am thankful that I was able to work as your Assistant Manger and that you continue to be a great mentor.

My book cover, logo, and business cards were all designed by the talented Kenya Gould, the owner of Kenya Designs. You were quick and excellent in all of your work. I couldn't have asked for a better designer and sister in faith. Your work speaks of your character, and it is beyond my own expectations. I look forward to future business with you as your business grows and others discover your talent.

I was lost with words, literally. My Publishing Coach Amanda Chambers, owner of Divine Legacy Publishing, LLC., I am thankful that the Author Bri Lynette introduced us to each other. You made all of this possible, and you were very helpful with assisting me in the process of becoming a self-published author. I admire your ability to step back from being a wife, mother, author, mentor, coach, business owner, and scholar. You motivate me to write more books and to strategically plan for the completion of my book.

To those who are no longer with us, to those who currently serve, and to those who have served while continuing to do so every day in our own country. Thank you for giving your time, dedication, and life for the liberty we enjoy each day.

To you. The person currently reading this book. Thank you for supporting me and for giving me a few moments of your life. Without you, I wouldn't have readers and for that, I am forever grateful. I hope that you find the time to write your own book of poems.

Allen L. Simmons is the founder of a 501(c)3 organization called Live N Love, Incorporated. After graduating high school he joined the United States Marine Corps with combat experience in Iraq and Afghanistan.

For the past five years, Allen has been known to be an influential part of his community and has used his platform to feed and clothe the homeless men and women of Charlotte. He gave multiple speeches at the Strategic Behavioral Health Center and has used his experiences from surviving war, PTSD, suicide, anxiety, and depression to inspire youth and employees.

Allen Simmons does not just have the ability to speak and inspire individuals; he is an inspiration. His story is one of overcoming and transformation.

Creative Control With Self-Publishing

Divine Legacy Publishing provides authors with the guid-ance necessary to take creative control of their work through self-publishing. We provide:

Writing Coaching

Professional Editing

Author Branding

Self-Publishing Coaching

Graphic Design

Website Design

Let Divine Legacy Publishing help you master the business of self-publishing.